Solving the Technology Challenge for IT Managers

Technologies That IT Managers Can Use In Order to Make Their Teams More Productive

"Practical, proven techniques that will help you to create highly productive IT teams"

Dr. Jim Anderson

Published by:
Blue Elephant Consulting
Tampa, Florida

Copyright © 2014 by Dr. Jim Anderson

All rights reserved. No part of this book may be reproduced of transmitted in any form or by any means, electronic or mechanical, including photocopying, recording or by any information storage and retrieval system without written permission of the publisher, except for inclusion of brief quotations in a review.

Printed in the United States of America

Library of Congress Control Number: 2014954042

ISBN-13: 978-1502829634

ISBN-10: 1502829630

Warning – Disclaimer

The purpose of this book is to educate and entertain. This book does not promise or guarantee that anyone following the ideas, tips, suggestions, techniques or strategies will be successful. The author, publisher and distributor(s) shall have neither liability nor responsibility to anyone with respect to any loss or damage caused, or alleged to be caused, directly or indirectly by the information contained in this book.

Recent Books by the Author

Product Management

- How Product Managers Can Grow Their Career: How Product Managers Can Find And Succeed In The Right Job

- Product Management Secrets: Techniques For Product Managers To Boost Product Sales And Increase Customer Satisfaction

Public Speaking

- Plan For Success: How To Plan Your Next Speech: How to plan a speech in order to achieve your goals and delight your audience

- How To Become A Better Speaker By Changing How You Speak: Change techniques that will transform a speech into a memorable event

CIO Skills

- Technology That Every CIO Needs To Know About: How CIOs Can Stay On Top Of the Changes in the Technology That Powers the Company

- What CIOs Need To Know About Working With Partners: Techniques For CIOs To Use In Order To Be Able To Successfully Work With

IT Manager Skills

- How IT Managers Can Make Innovation Happen: Tips And Techniques For IT Managers To Use In Order To Make Innovation Happen In Their Teams

- Secrets Of Effective Leadership For IT Managers: Tips And Techniques That IT Managers Can Use In Order To Develop Leadership Skills

Negotiating

- Learn How To Signal In Your Next Negotiation: How To Develop The Skill Of Effective Signaling In A Negotiation In Order To Get The Best Possible Outcome

- Learn The Skill Of Exploring In A Negotiation: How To Develop The Skill Of Exploring What Is Possible In A Negotiation In Order To Reach The Best Possible Deal

Miscellaneous

- The Internet-Enabled Successful School District Superintendent: How To Use The Internet To Boost Parental Involvement In Your Schools

- Power Distribution Unit (PDU) Secrets: What Everyone Who Works In A Data Center Needs To Know!

Note: See a complete list of books by Dr. Jim Anderson at the back of this book.

Acknowledgements

Any book like this one is the result of years of real-world work experience. In my over 25 years of working for 7 different firms, I have met countless fantastic people and I've been mentored by some truly exceptional ones. Although I've probably forgotten some of the people who made me the person that I am today, here is my attempt to finally give them the recognition that they so truly deserve:

- Thomas P. Anderson
- Art Puett
- Bobbi Marshall
- Bob Boggs

Dr. Jim Anderson

This book is dedicated to my family: Lori, Maddie, Nick, and Ben. None of this would have been possible without their constant love and support.

Thanks for always believing in me and providing me with the strength to always be willing to go out there and be my best for you.

Table of Contents

SOLVING THE TECHNOLOGY CHALLENGE FOR IT MANAGERS............8

ABOUT THE AUTHOR..10

CHAPTER 1: WEB 3.0 IS COMING – ARE IT LEADERS READY? 15

CHAPTER 2: MAYBE IT IS TIME FOR IT LEADERS TO GO SHOPPING TO LEARN NEW TRICKS 19

CHAPTER 3: WHAT A RENTAL CAR COMPANY CAN TEACH IT LEADERS 23

CHAPTER 4: SMOOTH CYBER-CRIMINALS: WHAT'S AN IT LEADER TO DO?..27

CHAPTER 5: A TALE OF WOE: WHAT TO DO WHEN IT IS TOO COMPLEX? 31

CHAPTER 6: JUST WHOSE JOB IS NETWORK SECURITY ANYWAY? 35

CHAPTER 7: IS ON-DEMAND THE RIGHT SOLUTION FOR YOUR IT TEAM? 38

CHAPTER 8: OPEN SOURCE: IS THIS A GOOD THING OR A BAD THING FOR IT?...41

CHAPTER 9: SECURE YOUR DATA AND BOOST YOUR CAREER 45

CHAPTER 10: WHY CLOUD COMPUTING WON'T WORK FOR EVERY IT PROJECT 49

CHAPTER 11: DO IT LEADERS (AND CEOS) HAVE THEIR HEADS STUCK IN THE CLOUD?..53

CHAPTER 12: IT MANAGERS NEED TO REALIZE THAT VIRTUALIZATION ISN'T ALL THAT IT'S CRACKED UP TO BE..57

Solving the Technology Challenge for IT Managers

As an IT manager you understand the value of technology. It's what provides our teams with the tools that we can use to accomplish great things for our company. The challenge that we run into is that technology is always changing.

This means that as an IT manager you have a responsibility to stay on top of all of the various technologies that your team will be called on to make use of. This includes Web 3.0 technologies, things that work in the world of retail shopping, and the latest developments in keeping those cyber criminals out of your company's networks.

Our jobs are by their very nature complex. We need to understand what the company expects of us – are we the ones who are responsible for securing the company network or does this task belong to someone else? As more and more services become available to us, we are the ones that the company will turn to in order to determine what on-demand services need to be acquired.

As we create solutions, we'll need to understand when open source solutions may provide us with the best technology. Cloud computing is a hot topic, but we need to be able to determine if it's right for our company. Finally, virtualization is currently in vogue but is it the right answer in every situation?

This book has been created to provide you with the insights into today's latest technologies that you are going to need in order to direct your team. The goal is to provide you with the knowledge that you are going to need in order to determine what technology to use in what situation.

For more information on what it takes to be a great IT manager, check out my blog, The Accidental IT Leader, at:

www.TheAccidentalITLeader.com

Good luck!

- Dr. Jim Anderson

About The Author

I must confess that I never set out to be a CIO. When I went to school, I studied Computer Science and thought that I'd get a nice job programming and that would be that. Well, at least part of that plan worked out!

My first job was working for Boeing on their F/A-18 fighter jet program. I spent my days programming fighter jet software in assembly language and I loved it. The U.S. government decided to save some money and went looking for other countries to sell this plane to. This put me into an unfamiliar role: I started to meet with foreign military officials and I ended up having to manage groups of engineers who were working on international projects.

Time moved on and so did I. I found myself working for Siemens, the big German telecommunications company. They were making phone switches and selling them to the seven U.S. phone companies. The problem was that the switches were too complicated. Customers couldn't tell the difference between one complicated phone switch from another complicated phone switch. Once again I found myself working with the sales and marketing teams to find ways to make the great technology that the engineers had developed understandable to both internal and external customers.

I've spent over 25 years working as a senior IT professional for both big companies and startups. This has given me an opportunity to learn what it takes to manage and IT department in ways that allow it to maximize its output while becoming a valuable part of the overall company.

I now live in Tampa Florida where I spend my time managing my consulting business, Blue Elephant Consulting, teaching college courses at the University of South Florida, and traveling to work with companies like yours to share the knowledge that I have about how to create and manage successful IT departments.

I'm always available to answer questions and I can be reached at:

Dr. Jim Anderson
Blue Elephant Consulting
Email: jim@BlueElephantConsulting.com
Facebook: http://goo.gl/1TVoK
Web: **www.BlueElephantConsulting.com**

"Unforgettable communication skills that will set your ideas free..."

Create IT Departments That Are Productive And A Valuable Asset To The Rest Of The Company!

Dr. Jim Anderson is available to provide training and coaching on the topics that are the most important to people who have to manage IT departments: how can I build a productive IT department (and keep it together) while at the same time providing the rest of the company with the IT services that they need?

Dr. Anderson believes that in order to both learn and remember what he says, speakers need to laugh. Each one of his speeches is full of fun and humor so that what he says "sticks" with everyone.

Dr. Anderson's CIO Skills Training Includes:

1. How to identify and attract the right type of IT workers to your IT department.
2. How to build relationships with the company's senior management in order to get the support that you need?
3. How to stay on top of changing technology and security issues so that you never get surprised?

Dr. Jim Anderson works with over 100 customers per year. To invite Dr. Anderson to work with you, contact him at:

Phone: 813-418-6970 or
Email: jim@BlueElephantConsulting.com

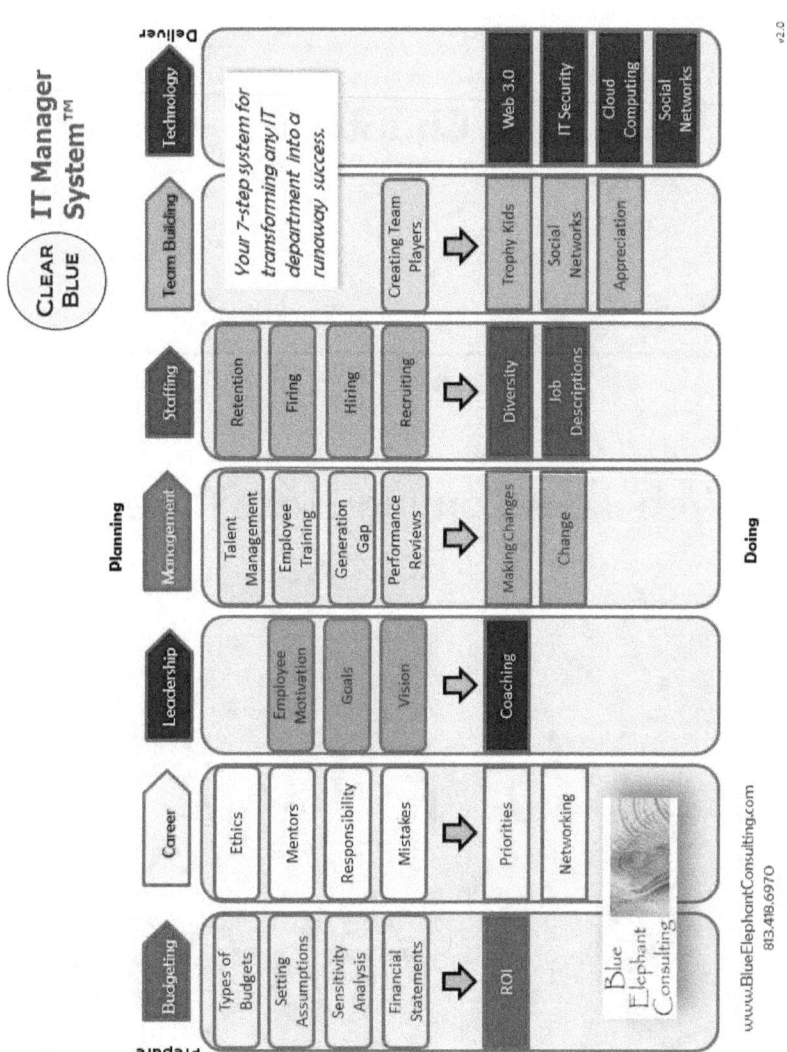

The **Clear Blue IT Manager System™** has been created to provide IT managers with a clear roadmap for how to manage an IT team. This system shows IT Managers what needs to be done and in what order to do it.

Chapter 1

Web 3.0 is Coming – Are IT Leaders Ready?

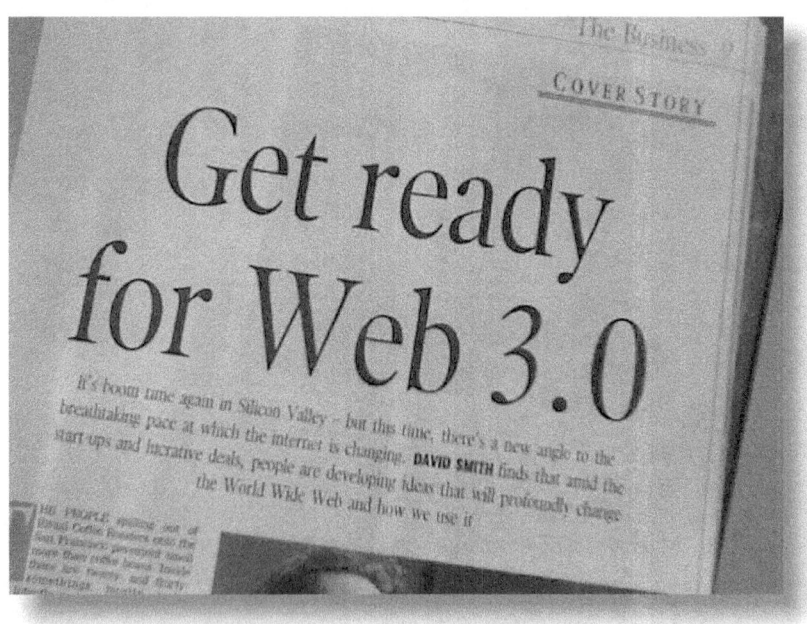

Chapter 1: Web 3.0 Is Coming – Are IT Leaders Ready?

Oh Web 2.0, it seems like only yesterday that you arrived – is it possible that already you may be getting ready to be replaced? The answer is not quite yet, but the outline of what the **Web 3.0** is going to look like is starting to firm up. IT Leaders need to start getting ready for this change now so that when it arrives they can take advantage of all that it will offer…

What Was Web 2.0?

Before we run off and start making predictions about the future of the Internet, maybe it would be a good idea to take just a moment and make sure that we are all on the same page as to just exactly **what the Web 2.0 is / was.**

When the web first showed up (Web 1.0), everyone rushed out and created static web pages. That was a great start, but it got a bit boring because nothing changed without a great deal of effort. Web 2.0 extended what we had by adding blogging, **Wikipedia**, social networking (**MySpace**, **Facebook**, **LinkedIn**, etc.) and even microblogging (**Twitter**). This changed everything because all of a sudden things could be easily changed – and they were!

What Is Web 3.0 Going To Be?

IT Leaders who are trying to keep their teams on track and on top of new technologies need to be asking just what is going to make up the Web 3.0. Dr. Jim Hendler at the Rensselaer Polytechnic Institute has been spending some time thinking about this and he's come up with some interesting ideas. Dr. Hendler points out that the next version of the Web appears to all be based on **Tim Berners-Lee's** (you know, the guy who invented the Web) vision of a semantic web.

In this next iteration of the web, what we're going to see is more and more complex **mashups of data** from different applications being used to deliver data in more useful ways. Dr. Hendler believes that the read-write abilities of Web 2.0 applications will be used to build Web 3.0 applications that operate at the data, not the application, level.

What's Going to Make the Web 3.0 Happen?

Before the Web 3.0 can show up, a few critical pieces need to drop into place. Ultimately, what needs to happen is that it has to become easier to integrate web data resources. This is exactly what IT Leaders need to be staying on top of. Here are the **emerging technologies** that are going to allow this to happen:

- **Resource Description Framework (RDF)**: provides a means to link data from multiple different websites or databases. Uses the SQL-like SPARQL query language.

- **Uniform Resource Identifiers (URI)**: We already have these – this is how you merge and map data that is found in different locations on the web.

- **Web Ontology Language (OWL)**: allows relationships to be inferred between data that is stored in different parts of the same application.

Final Thoughts

IT Leaders have many different responsibilities that they have to juggle at the same time. Keeping up on new and emerging technologies is part of the job. The Web 3.0 will be at least as significant of a change as the Web 2.0 was. If they move quickly, IT Leaders can position their teams to get in front of a **significant change** before it happens. Right now they have such a chance – Web 3.0 is not here yet, but it's getting ready to arrive.

IT Leaders need to have their teams spending time to understand what problems that the company is facing today will be able to be solved once you have a better way to unify all of that data that is available on the web. A critical first step is assigning staff to learn and become experts on the new **Web 3.0 technologies** early on. If you can prepare for the future AND accomplish your other IT tasks at the same time, then the Web 3.0 will have provided you with yet another way to transform yourself from an IT manager into a **true leader**.

Chapter 2

Maybe it is Time for IT Leaders to Go Shopping to Learn New Tricks

Chapter 2: Maybe it is Time for IT Leaders to Go Shopping to Learn New Tricks

Good IT Leaders find ways to use the tools that IT provides along with the skills that their teams have in order to help the company **move faster and do more.** Nowhere is this currently more visible than in the world of retail sales…

Do Retail Stores Even Still Exist?

After the past bruising few years, one might be forgiven for thinking that the world of retail was going away. Look around and you can probably see countless shuttered stores in your area. However, if you take a moment and look just a bit closer you'll see something else: **some stores are starting to wake up.** The global recession drove a lot of firms out of business, but the ones that are left are eager to get back to work.

Their products haven't really changed all that much, but they realize that they are going to have to work hard to **change the shopping experience** for their beaten-down customers. Making shopping easy is the goal and this is where IT Leaders can lend a helping hand.

The research firm IDC forecasted that worldwide retail IT spending was going to grow by 2.4% from $81B to $83B in 2009. On the flip side in the manufacturing sector, they forecasted that supply chain management spending was going to grow to $3B in 2009. Clearly retail firms are **placing their bets for future growth** in the hands of their IT departments.

What Can IT Leaders Do To Help Online Stores?

Being willing to help the company out is an important part of being an IT Leader in retail; however, often times the big question is **just where that help is needed**. The first thing to realize is that not all stores are created equal. Specifically, online stores are different from traditional bricks & mortar stores.

If you work for an online store, then you are going to want to be using your team's IT talents to find ways to **add more features to your web sites**. These can include such things as: making purchasing easier, adding customer reviews, or even videos showing how to use your products.

Online stores are lucky (sort of) in that they have a great role model in their industry: Amazon.com. Love 'em or hate 'em, everyone agrees that Amazon does **a great job** of presenting products and then selling them like there's no tomorrow.

Following Amazon's lead, IT Leaders need to work with their teams to find ways to **simplify the online checkout process** and incorporate recommendation engines that can help solve customer problems while up-selling additional products.

What Can IT Leaders Do To Help Offline Stores?

Traditional stores that were not **"Internet only"** stores were predicted to be going away now that the Internet has arrived. However, clearly that's not happening. Instead, what's going on is that traditional stores are using IT to reinvent themselves and make the shopping experience more enjoyable for their customers.

Moving the point-of-sale (POS) terminals to **where the customers are** is one way that IT Leaders and their teams can help out the rest of the business. In order to do this a whole series of IT challenges need to be overcome such as finding ways to wirelessly connect cash registers to the network and allow credit cards to be securely processed.

Inventory management and its cousin application supply chain management are also prime areas where IT can help traditional retailers to reduce costs and boost profits. Implementing or optimizing these applications allows a retailer to link their sales forecasts with their manufacturing or ordering processes and prevents over / under stocks.

What All of This Means for You

If IT Leaders aren't careful they can **focus on the wrong things**. They can spend too much time thinking about how to optimize what IT does, and not enough time thinking about how to make the rest of the business run better.

Online and offline retailers are **different types of firms**. IT can play a role in helping both types of companies be more successful by helping them to make the customer's shopping experience more enjoyable.

IT lives to serve the rest of the business. This means that smart IT Leaders know that when it comes to supporting a retail business, it's how they use IT that's going to be the key to their success.

Chapter 3

What a Rental Car Company Can Teach IT Leaders

Chapter 3: What a Rental Car Company Can Teach IT Leaders

As IT Leaders, we should all be trying harder to find ways to use the talents of our teams to make our companies run smoother. Hmm, I wonder if there are any companies out there that could serve as an example for us? Good news – there is one: Avis Rent A Car.

How Hard Can It Be To Rent A Car?

It turns out that Avis Rent A Car is really both Avis and Budget – both companies are owned by the same company (who knew?) The first lesson that IT Leaders can learn from Avis is how they roll out new technologies: they don't bet the farm on any one technology. Instead they do proof-of-concept trials and gauge customer feedback in order to decide if they should go ahead and rollout a solution company-wide.

Avis is not afraid to use wireless technology if it solves a problem. If you've returned a rental car to Avis lately, you've probably been greeted by an employee standing in the return line with a wireless device. I know that I haven't had to go into the office to return a car in a long time – thank you wireless (great because I always seem to be running late for my plane).

As an example of IT Leaders thinking outside of the box, Avis has taken this remote check in one step further and now they will email you a copy of your receipt so that you don't have to worry about stuffing a piece of paper into your luggage as you jump on the shuttle bus.

How to Innovate When You Work In a Parking Lot

One of the reasons that Avis' IT Leaders are so innovative is because they can see their competition on the other side of the parking lot. That causes them to try harder.

The Avis data center is currently outsourced to IBM so Avis doesn't have to spend any time worrying about typical data center activities. Instead they spend their time working on things like trying to make sure that a customer's experience at the rental counter will be the same experience that they'll have when they visit the company's web sites.

The Internet plays a big part in every IT shop these days and Avis is no different. Avis uses XML to interface to other travel related businesses via the Internet. By doing this they are able to avoid booking fees and this saves everyone a lot of money.

Finally, Avis IT Leaders have also spent a lot of time and effort to create a direct connection between themselves and their insurance companies, car dealerships, and collision repair shops. This allows them to quickly react whenever one of their customers has a car crash.

What All of This Means for You

Normally rental car companies and their cars don't get even a second glance from IT Leaders as we race though the airport. However, maybe we've been overlooking a well-run IT shop in our haste.

Avis is locked in a constant struggle with other rental car companies, so their IT Leaders have to be constantly innovating. They use whatever IT technology best suits the issue that they are trying to solve and this includes wireless and XML.

In the end, it's the close working relationship that the Avis IT Leaders have been able to create between themselves and the business side of the house that has allowed them to achieve so much. Maybe that's why they try harder…

Chapter 4

Smooth Cyber-Criminals: What's an IT Leader to Do?

Chapter 4: Smooth Cyber-Criminals: What's An IT Leader to Do?

If you were a bank manager and all of sudden one day armed and masked criminals walked in through the bank's front door and demanded money, what would you do? I can think of a whole bunch of possible options, many of them suggested by countless action movies. The key point here is that you sure wouldn't just sit there and do nothing. So why, as cyber criminals target your company's IT infrastructure, are you just sitting there today?

What's Missing?

Hey, you're just an IT Leader right? You spend your days trying to get a team of IT professionals to work together to accomplish great things for the company, who's got time to worry about **cyber criminals** coming in from the outside? Well guess what, just like preventing forest fires, stopping cyber-crime is everyone's job.

In most IT departments and the companies that they are part of, what's missing is **a companywide strategy** for dealing with the twin issues of system security and regulatory compliance. One of the key reasons that we seem to do such a poor job of this is simply because nobody's really been trained on what the best way to identify and classify risk is.

If you think about it, the threats come from **a wide variety of different sources**: smart international cyber criminals, angry ex-employees, and everyday user mistakes and gullibility.

The Bad Guys Just Keep Getting Badder

Every IT Leader needs to always **be on the alert** for things that just don't seem right. It can be as simple as members of your team's laptops not behaving in a way that they are supposed to or you receiving suspicious phishing phone calls.

The experts who study the ways of modern cyber criminals are telling us that the bad guys have recently really started to take it up a notch. They are **evolving** from the cyber equivalent of petty street crime to mob-like activities.

What's going on now is that cyber criminals are **taking over control** of large numbers of PCs (creating what's called a "botnet") and then remotely commanding them to take synchronized actions that can do things like take down web sites. They take advantage of major news stories such as earthquakes and convince people to download software that then infects their computer.

What's An IT Leader to Do?

Great, so the world is evolving and becoming a more dangerous place for IT Leaders to work and play, this naturally leads to the interesting question: **what should you be doing about it?**

As an IT Leader, you have a single way of making your company more secure: **managing your IT team**. You need to be doing the following three things: making sure that your team is constantly being trained and educated about the latest threats, restricting the types of applications and corporate data that each member of your team has access to, and finally making sure that when an employee leaves for whatever reason that you firmly lock all of the system doors after them.

What All of This Means for You

IT Leaders already have a full plate of things to do. However, it turns out that the forces of cyber darkness continue to grow and become more dangerous to companies. This means that **everyone has a role to play in keeping the company safe from outside threats**.

As an IT Leader you have a responsibility to make sure that your team is **part of the solution, not part of the problem**. This means that you need to work with your team to boost their awareness of cyber threats and make sure that they don't get tempted to harm the company.

By doing your part to secure the company against cyber criminals, you'll be freeing your team from potential distractions and outages and in the end; **you're going to be making everyone more successful**.

Chapter 5

A Tale of Woe: What to Do When IT is Too Complex?

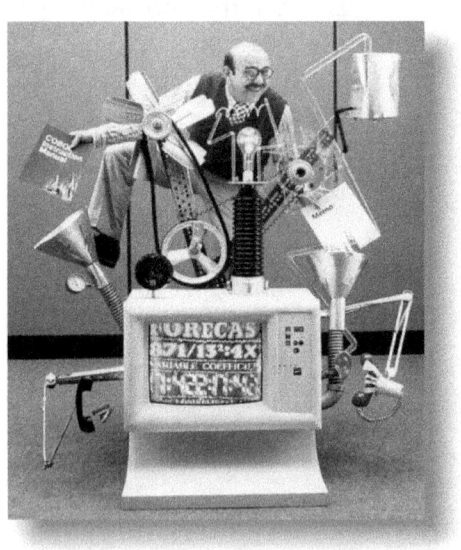

Chapter 5: A Tale Of Woe: What To Do When IT Is Too Complex?

There probably isn't a problem out there that couldn't be solved by adding some IT to it. In fact, once you had done that, you could probably make that solution even better by adding more IT to it. At what point is too much IT considered to be **too much of a good thing**? IT Leaders need to be able to realize when enough is enough...

The Story of a (Small) Bank

Doug Bartholomew has taken the time to hunt down stories about when IT Leaders allowed **the technology monster to get out of its cage**. One such story has to do with a small bank in Texas that had a pretty simple problem: they wanted to keep track of all of their interactions with their customers.

Now any IT Leader worth their salt would instantly realize that this type of customer issue is exactly what **Customer Relationship Management (CRM)** software packages have been designed for. The trick; however, is to match the solution to the problem – and that didn't happen here.

The small bank had 16 bankers who kept track of everything on paper. It was working ok, but they had difficulty "seeing" just how much contact they were having with a given customer. Everyone agreed that a CRM solution was needed. In the end, the bank selected a **Siebel Systems** (now a part of Oracle) solution.

Did You Hear The One About The Monster Application…?

There's no question that Siebel makes a great CRM application. I mean it sure seems like it can do just about everything. The problem in this case is that the small bank **really didn't want it to do everything**: most of the installation of the application focused on turning off functionality that they didn't want.

The next issue was the simple fact that for a customer who didn't have a lot of existing technology, the solution that they selected came across as being very complex. Multiple screens had to be navigated to complete a function and **a new way of thinking** about both products and customers had to be adopted.

The result of this is that the very folks that the bank needed to use the new system, the bankers, **didn't want anything to do with it**. Once they stopped using it, the value of the application to the bank pretty much went out the door.

In the end, after having invested **roughly $500,000** in software licenses and implementation costs, the bank ended up walking away from their CRM application.

A New Way of Doing Business

This story might end on a sad note with the bank staff going back to doing everything by hand, but it doesn't. Instead, the IT Leaders went out and **found another application** that better suited their needs. This new application was much simpler although it had a lot less functionality. It was just a shared database and spreadsheet program that was much easier for the bankers to use.

In fact, the bankers soon found that they were able to **create customized reports** without having to ask IT to help do it. Now that's using IT the way that it's supposed to be used!

What All of This Means for You

IT Leaders do **love our IT technology**. However, we need to keep in mind that not every business problem that comes up needs to be solved with an ultra-sophisticated IT application.

We always have to take the time before we design an IT solution to **study our customers**: what is their real issue? The trick to creating the right IT solution is to provide the end user with just enough (but not too much) IT technology to get their job done.

IT Leaders who can take the time and **not over design solutions for their end users** are the ones who will be able to best meet the company's goals of doing more and moving faster using IT technology.

Chapter 6

Just Whose Job is Network Security Anyway?

Chapter 6: Just Whose Job Is Network Security Anyway?

IT Leaders hope to be able to do their work **in a secure environment** – the last thing that any of us want to have to worry about is dealing with an attack on our servers or network from bad guys. However, have you ever stopped to wonder just whose job it is to keep everything secure?

How Goes The Battle?

Everyone in IT knows that there is a constant struggle going on **between the good guys and the bad guys**. The larger the company that you work for, the more often you'll be attacked. This means that you need to be playing your role in helping the rest of the company constantly reevaluate its security policies.

If you need some good news, here it is: most companies are getting better at dealing with the IT monsters that we now recognize – worms, viruses, and others. The bad news is that the threats continue to evolve and mutate. **The bad guys just keep getting smarter**.

Who's The Target?

Should you even be worrying about this? I mean, look, you've got enough on your plate already – do you really have to deal with this? The folks over at CIO Insite did a survey awhile back and found out that 50% of companies that are big (revenue of over $1B) have said that their web sites and corporate data **have been targeted by the bad guys**.

What Should Your Role Be?

This is where things start to get tricky. For you see, everyone in IT really has **a role to play** in keeping the company's IT assets secure. How an IT Leader goes about doing this can have a big impact on both their career as well as how secure the company is.

All too often, a company exists in **react mode**. We've all see how this plays out. An attack from the outside will be detected and then as many IT staffers who can be roped in are thrown into the mix in order to take the servers that are being attacked off line, make sure that all of the needed patches have been applied to the other servers, and then keep an eye out on the rest of the network in order to detect any unusual going ons.

As IT Leaders we need to realize that is exactly the wrong way to go about doing these things. What is needed is more of **an automated approach** to keeping the company's severs, web sites, and network secure. The right way to do this is to establish standard procedures as well as a consistent set of company policies that get implemented in order to make sure that all of your security updates are in place. This is the key to stopping the "we're under attack" madness.

What All of This Means for You

Although your firm may have **an IT team dedicated to network security**, it is still the responsibility of every IT Leader to lend a hand in helping to keep the bad guys out.

Just exactly how to go about doing this is **different at every company**. In the worst case, it can mean lending a hand when an attack on the firm's IT resources is detected. However, the smart IT Leaders deal with the problem before it shows up and create automated ways to keep IT resources secure.

Chapter 7

Is On-Demand the Right Solution for Your IT Team?

Chapter 7: Is On-Demand the Right Solution for Your IT Team?

If you've been reading any of the trade press over the last couple of years, you have undoubtedly run across story after story that talked about the next big thing in IT: on-demand computing. I'm willing to bet that members of your IT team may be clambering to take your next project "into the cloud". Sure **it sounds sexy**, but should you do it...?

It's all about the Upside

Look, haven't we all **finally figured out how to do all of this IT stuff the right way?** Why would any IT Leader in their right mind even consider using an on-demand solution when they are creating their next enterprise project?

The upside of moving your team's efforts to using an on-demand IT architecture are pretty powerful: **much lower hardware requirements** (for you, maybe not so for the on-demand provider!), a drop in software development costs, and simplifying the always-present challenge of how you can update an application that is used by lots and lots of employees. Having a single version of an application that exists on an on-demand system sure seems to be the right way to go. Or is it...?

...But Then There's That Downside

Pesky issues such as **reliability** keep popping up when IT Leaders start to talk about on-demand based IT solutions. What are your customers going to do if the on-demand system can't be reached? Oh and how long is this down time going to last...?

Can anyone say **"customization"**? When you have a single version of an application running in an on-demand environment your end users will by necessity lose at least some of their ability to customize the application. Is this a big deal? It all depends on how big of an impact on productivity that customization had...

No man is an island and the same thing can be said for your IT applications. It turns out that **integrating** an on-demand application into all of those other applications that the company is using can be a tough nut to crack. Yes it can be done, but no it's not going to be easy.

What All of This Means for You

For those of you who were looking for **a silver bullet solution** and thought that you had found it in the on-demand design, sorry. Yes there are benefits, but these come with some serious costs.

Getting out of the business of having to worry about what hardware your solutions are running on and where they are located **would be a great feeling**. However, you then start to have a brand new set of reliability and integration issues that show up.

In the end, **on-demand is here to stay** and just based on the cost savings that it delivers alone it's going to be the right solution for certain IT challenges. However, it's the wise IT Leader who pauses before jumping into the on-demand lake and makes sure that it's the right decision for right now...

Chapter 8

Open Source: Is This a Good Thing or a Bad Thing for IT?

Chapter 8: Open Source: Is This A Good Thing Or A Bad Thing For IT?

What if software was free? Every IT Leader has to stop and ask themselves this question every once in a while. With the cost of ERP and database systems constantly increasing, software costs can quickly become a significant expense for any IT department. The **"Open Source" software movement**, born in the days when Napster was giving away commercial music for free, is one way the IT departments can get high quality software for free. But should they?

The Many Flavors of Open Source

There isn't enough space in this article to list all of the open source projects and applications that are out there. Some of the more famous include the **LAMP stack (Linux, Apache, MySQL, and Python).** In my business I use WordPress to blog and vTiger for CRM; however, there is also the Movable Type platform and SugarCRM to choose from.

A healthy open source project has **lots of programmers** contributing changes and new features to it. It needs strong central management in order to do good project management: what goes into the next release, who tests it, and when it's available for general release.

Why IT Leaders Should Use Open Source

When an IT Leader considers using open source applications as a part of an IT project, **support** is the first thought that springs to mind. In the world of Linux this issue has been solved by the arrival of multiple firms that provide professional support for given flavors of Linux distro (Redhat, etc.).

If an open source package is popular, there will be a firm out there that can provide support for it. However, one of the unique aspects of the open source movement is that there is a very large **unofficial support group** for virtually every application. On countless web sites and support boards, IT staffers who run into a problem with an open source application can post their issues. Eager users and volunteer programmers will more often than not spring into action and provide quick suggestions on how to solve the problem.

One additional benefit of using open source is that it gives an IT Leader a way to **motivate and retain staff**. Allowing your members of your team to work on an open source project and to contribute new features that they develop to the overall project can be a fantastic motivational tool. This allows them to feel that they are contributing to a worthwhile cause. Happy workers don't want to leave their team.

Why IT Leaders Should Not Use Open Source

You'd think that the case for using open source was open and shut, right? I mean after all it's free. However, before you leap you may want to **double think** taking that plunge.

For one thing, the road today is littered with open source projects that were born, flourished for a while, and then **died due to lack of interest**. It truly does take a village to keep one of these things going and if you've based a mission critical process on an open source app that dies, then you may be left high and dry.

Support is another issue. The concept of having **"one throat to choke"** is one thing that helps IT Leaders sleep well at night. If you are using open source, then there may be no responsible party for you to reach out to if all of a sudden things stop working.

Your specific IT configuration **may no longer be supported** at some point in time: if the rest of the world moves on to the next version of an operating system and it's not yet time for you to do so, your open source apps may stop working.

Finally, the more time that your team spends working on open source apps, **the more transferable their job skills may become**. They may decide to pick up and move on after they've gained the knowledge that you paid them to learn.

What All of This Means for You

For IT Leaders, the world of open source software keeps getting **even larger and more established** than it is today. You are going to have to make some hard decisions as to just how far into the open source pond you are willing to wade with your team.

Open source often comes with **little or no formal support**. However, the sheer number of people working on a project can fill in the gaps. Allowing your team to work on open source projects can be a double edged sword: they'll have more job satisfaction, but they might end up leaving.

The price of open source software really isn't free – **you'll have to make an investment in it if you want to use it**. Pick wisely and you just might become known as the open IT Leader.

Chapter 9

Secure Your Data and Boost Your Career

Chapter 9: Secure Your Data and Boost Your Career

I guess I could have used a different title also "Make Your Data Unsecure and Sink Your Career"! Although IT Leaders spend much of their time worrying about making sure that their IT teams are working together to be successful, that pesky issue of data security keeps creeping into everything that we do. Maybe it's time for you to make a plan...

What You Are Doing Wrong Right Now

One of the keys to having a successful IT Leader career is to not get caught up in some big data breach incident – it's hard for an IT career to recover from something like that. Even fancy new IT trends like cloud computing won't save the day – it just means all of your valuable stuff is in one place for the hackers to attack.

Right now too many IT Leaders' approach to securing their company's data is to realize that they've got a bunch of valuable data sitting on a bunch of servers inside of some data center. Their approach is to install guards (firewalls) and to limit how people can gain access to the data (intrusion detection systems). Although this is a necessary step, it's not nearly enough.

The Right Way to Do Data Security

So if we know what the wrong (or at least incomplete) way to do data security is, what should IT Leaders be doing? Simply put, you need a new security strategy.

The goal is pretty straightforward. You should be able to protect both your structured and unstructured data no matter where it is: being used by both employees and customers, stored on a network file systems, or as it's in flight over the network.

What we're really talking about is doing away with the old idea of an IT information security program and instead replacing it with an enterprise risk management program.

What Are The Right Questions To Ask?

Michael Davis is a security consultant who has taken a look at this issue and he believes that there are four questions that need to be asked by the person who owns each piece of corporate data:

- Where is the data?
- What exactly is the data?
- Who has access to the data?
- Why do they need to have access to it?

Taking the time to ask, answer, and remember what the answer was to these questions is the key to developing a sound corporate data security program.

Who Should Be In Charge?

The final question that you need an answer to is just exactly who should have the ultimate responsibility for the security of your data? Interestingly enough, the answer does not lie in IT.

Instead, the experts recommend that a non-technical business-side owner be selected and vested with the power to make all decisions regarding the data in question. By doing it this way, you can ensure that the business value of the data being secured will be part of any decision regarding how to secure it.

What All of This Means for You

IT Leaders walk a fine line: they need to complete their IT projects as quickly as possible and yet at the same time they need to take the time to make sure that corporate data remains secure. The old ways of doing this are no longer enough.

IT security programs are morphing to become part of a larger enterprise risk management program. Assigning a non-IT person to be responsible for making decisions about a given type of corporate data is the first step. The next step is to make sure that the right questions are being asked.

You can never completely guard against a hacker breaking in and attacking your data. However, smart IT Leaders know that with the right responsible parties and by asking the right questions, it is possible to do a good job of securing the data that needs to be secured.

Chapter 10

Why Cloud Computing Won't Work for Every IT Project

Chapter 10: Why Cloud Computing Won't Work For Every IT Project

If IT was a game show and you were a contestant on it, right now it sure seems as though you could correctly any question that you were asked by replying "cloud computing". That's because cloud computing, basically outsourcing parts of your next IT project's IT infrastructure and applications, sure seems like a great idea. However, early reports back from the front lines by other IT Leaders are starting to paint a different picture...

...And Why Are We Talking About Clouds?

The reason that we're talking about cloud computing is because it's ushered in an era of "software as a service", or SaaS if you want to be cool. The reason that IT Leaders like to talk about SaaS based applications that run in the cloud is because they offer an opportunity to save the company a lot of money.

A single user's subscription to a SaaS application generally costs an IT Leader about $10 – $50 per month. The beauty of this approach is that that cost includes maintenance, support, and even the hardware that the application runs on. Oh, and all of a sudden your users can log into the application from anywhere – they don't have to be in the office to do work.

Just How Big Of A Deal Is This?

SaaS (and Cloud Computing) is growing like a weed right now. The folks over at Gartner are telling us that in the business software market, SaaS offerings make up about 9% of what's out there right now and it's expected to hit 16% by 2013 because it's growing at about 20% per year.

This is where IT Leaders are starting to see problems pop up. Since the whole SaaS market is growing so fast, even the people who work in it are finding themselves unable to keep up. This means that IT Leaders who are trying to get information on what products are available are starting to run into sales people who really don't know what their company's product can and cannot do. This is where problems with SaaS offerings start...

What's Wrong with SaaS?

Unlike the glowing brochures that you'll get from SaaS providers and the industry rag articles that are falling over themselves saying that Cloud Computing is the "next big thing", IT Leaders who are on the front lines are reporting that SaaS is not a silver bullet and has its own set of problems.

In fact, some companies that went down the SaaS route are now pulling back. Gartner reports that the top reasons that IT Leaders have been deciding to discontinue their SaaS deployments are:

- Difficulty in integration with existing applications
- High cost of services
- Lack of agility provided to the business
- Level of investment required
- Lack of robustness
- Poor track record of provider
- Poor client references
- Inadequate security, privacy, or confidentiality
- Didn't meet technical requirements
- Bottom Line Issues

In the end, it all comes down to money. One of the biggest attractions of SaaS is that it offers hard-pressed IT Leaders a way to stretch their IT project budgets farther. However, IT

Leaders that have implemented SaaS solutions are reporting that the benefits may not be so clear after all.

In the initial years, yes – your IT project will save on having to make the big CapEx investments that they would normally have to make in order to create the infrastructure to support another enterprise application. However, what seems to be missing is the ultimate reduction in people to support that solution and infrastructure costs over time.

What All of This Means for You

The world of IT keeps changing all the time and as an IT Leader you're going to have to move fast in order to keep up. SaaS offers many benefits; however, the drawbacks are also starting to show up.

IT Leaders on the frontlines of SaaS deployments are reporting that they are running into issues with integrating the SaaS applications with their existing enterprise applications. Additionally, many of the economic benefits appear to be only in the first few years with the long term benefits not being nearly as clear.

Right now Cloud Computing and SaaS are hot topics that every IT Leader should be looking into. However, look before you leap as the saying goes...

Chapter 11

Do IT Leaders (and CEOs) Have Their Heads Stuck in the Cloud?

Chapter 11: Do IT Leaders (and CEOs) Have Their Heads Stuck In The Cloud?

Ok, enough of this cloud stuff already! The field of IT is just like every other field out there and we have our own share of trendy topics – cloud computing sure seems to the one that we're dealing with right now. With all of the magazine articles on clouds and conferences going on, you'd think that every IT Leader and CEO has a good understanding of just exactly what a cloud is. Well, you'd be wrong...

Everybody Thinks That Clouds Are Important

In order to be a successful IT Leader, you're going to have to have the support of your firm's Senior Management. I guess one good thing is that it's become clear that firm's senior management have been reading the headlines and actually recognize the term "cloud computing". Mark McDonald over at Gartner has been asking around to find out just how deep this knowledge goes.

Back in 2009 (was it really that long ago?) only about 5% of a firm's senior management recognized the term. That's popped up to 37% these days (remember that not everyone works in IT!)

To take this one step further, they also appear to know that cloud computing is important. Those senior managers now list cloud computing as being one of their top 5 IT priorities.

One Out Of Three Isn't Bad, Is It?

Good IT Leaders understand that in the field of IT, there is no such thing as just one magical technology. Instead, solutions to difficult business challenges are built using multiple IT technologies that all have to work together.

The same level of understanding about how the world of IT works is not shared by the rest of most firms' senior management. Mark McDonald's research shows that too little is fully understood about how cloud computing really works. Clouds are built using three separate pieces of IT technology:

- Server Virtualization
- Service Orientated Architecture (SOA)
- Software as a Service (SaaS)

In order to implement a cloud solution, firms need to adopt all three technologies. However, this point has not yet sunk in with most non-IT senior management.

Gartner's research shows that most executives have very little interest in any of these technologies despite their belief that cloud computing is the way for their IT departments to go. Furthermore, roughly half of the executives surveyed believed that virtualization alone was the same thing as cloud computing.

What's Next for Clouds?

Well, at least they all know that cloud computing exists and that's got to be a good thing, right? Actually, no. Studies of new and emerging IT technologies have shown that they all seem to follow a predictable path.

Right now, most members of your firm's senior management team are probably quite excited about the potential of cloud computing. Soon, this will change. As it becomes clear that this isn't a magical cure (and cost reducer) that will solve all of your firm's problems, cloud computing will move into what Gartner calls "the trough of disillusionment". This is when people reject a novel new technology because it didn't live up to its initial hype.

What All of This Means for You

IT Leaders understand the true power of cloud computing. It offers a way to efficiently scale a firm's computing infrastructure while at the same time allowing it to keep its IT operational costs under control.

Realizing that your senior management doesn't quite fully "get" what cloud computing is and that they'll soon decide that its not all that it was touted to be is an important understanding that we all need to have.

IT Leaders are going to have to continue to focus on finding ways to make use of cloud computing resources while incorporating its supporting technologies into the projects that they are working on today. Cloud computing will eventually arrive on the IT scene and it's up to you to be ready when it comes.

Chapter 12

IT Managers Need to Realize that Virtualization Isn't All That It's Cracked Up to Be

Chapter 12: IT Managers Need to Realize that Virtualization Isn't All That It's Cracked Up to Be

To read the IT trade journals or speak with IT managers you'd think that we've all found the magic silver bullet that IT's been looking for during the past few years: **server virtualization**. The ability to mash together a bunch of different expensive individual servers and shrink the company's IT footprint down by a factor of 5x while reducing power and cooling costs at the same time sure seems to be a miracle cure for IT budget problems. Guess what: this isn't Hogwarts and you're not Harry Potter. Virtualization has its own set of problems and we need to have a talk...

What Is Virtualization?

So first off, let's make sure that we're all on the same page here with our understanding of just exactly what this virtualization thing is. In the past, IT teams used to **set up a new server** for each new application that they wanted to deploy. This resulted in the team having to maintain farms of servers that were all horribly underutilized.

The arrival of virtualization software changed everything. This low level software allowed **multiple applications** to run on the same physical hardware but believe that they had the box all to themselves. Now you could combine multiple individual servers into a single physical box. Things like what operating system an application used no longer mattered – you could mix and match to your heart's content.

Problem: Virtual Machine Sprawl

Evangelos Kotsovinos has taken a close look at just exactly what it means to introduce **lots of virtual machines** into a company's IT infrastructure. What he's found is that although IT managers might think that this changes everything, it doesn't.

It turns out that managing a virtual machine (VM) takes roughly **the same amount of effort** that managing a real box does. When you couple this with the fact that it has become so easy to set up new VMs, what you're seeing is unconstrained virtual machine sprawl.

IT teams are struggling to keep up with more and more VMs as staff set them up and then forget about them. Every IT manager now needs to come up with **a VM reclamation solution**.

Problem: Scaling

The very newness of VMs is causing IT teams to encounter **a whole new set of management headaches**. In the old days, IT teams had developed the tools and processes that they needed in order to deal with building large groups of new servers or handling a planned data center maintenance activity.

The arrival of VMs has upset this carefully established way of doing things. The problem is that often the VM management tools aren't able to **scale up** to the size of enterprise operations. This leaves IT teams struggling to find ways to manage the beast that they have created.

Problem: Troubleshooting

There's something deeply satisfying about tackling a system problem when you have the physical box in front of you. You know that you can always reach out and **swap out** various components if you have to. The same is not true when you've virtualized all of your servers.

Kotsovinos points out that a VM is really a collection of **interconnected physical subsystems**: server, storage, and network. When you are dealing with a system problem, like a slowdown, it's going to require a whole new set of skills to track down what's really going on. Additionally, virtualization is so new that often the right tools to do this type of trouble shooting may not exist yet.

Problem: Silos

Think about how your teams are set up today. Generally we draw lines **between various disciplines** based on what they do: the UNIX team, the Windows team, the storage guys, the network guys, etc. The arrival of virtualization in the data center is going to screw all of this up.

The reason that virtualization can cause such a disruption is because issues that have to do with the VMs more often than not **involve all of the various disciplines**. No longer will the storage team be able to just focus on storage issues. Instead, they are going to have to work together with several other teams in order to try to solve complex problems.

What All of This Means for You

Server virtualization is **a fantastic discovery**. However, IT Managers need to realize that it's not going to make all of their problems go away.

Instead, virtualization is going to end up **replacing** one set of problems with another. These will include potentially unchecked virtual machine sprawl, scaling issues, more challenging troubleshooting, and a breakdown in the IT silo structure.

Face it; virtualization is going to take over both the IT back office and probably the IT front office eventually. IT Managers need to understand that as this occurs, we're all going to have to **adjust how IT teams are run** in order to meet the new set of demands that virtualization is going to put on us…

It's from the forge of failure that the steel of success is formed.

Hard Work Does Not Guarantee Success, But Success Does Not Happen Without Hard Work.

- **Dr. Jim Anderson**

Create IT Departments That Are Productive And A Valuable Asset To The Rest Of The Company!

Dr. Jim Anderson is available to provide training and coaching on the topics that are the most important to people who have to manage IT departments: how can I build a productive IT department (and keep it together) while at the same time providing the rest of the company with the IT services that they need?

Dr. Anderson believes that in order to both learn and remember what he says, speakers need to laugh. Each one of his speeches is full of fun and humor so that what he says "sticks" with everyone.

Dr. Anderson's CIO Skills Training Includes:

1. How to identify and attract the right type of IT workers to your IT department.
2. How to build relationships with the company's senior management in order to get the support that you need?
3. How to stay on top of changing technology and security issues so that you never get surprised?

Dr. Jim Anderson works with over 100 customers per year. To invite Dr. Anderson to work with you, contact him at:

Phone: 813-418-6970 or
Email: jim@BlueElephantConsulting.com

Photo Credits:

Cover – By: Keoni Cabral
https://www.flickr.com/photos/keoni101/

Chapter 1 - By: Peter Asquith
https://www.flickr.com/photos/wasabicube/

Chapter 2 - By: Caden Crawford
https://www.flickr.com/photos/cadencrawford/

Chapter 3 - By: 1950s Unlimited
https://www.flickr.com/photos/blakta2/

Chapter 4 - By: Vincent Desjardins
https://www.flickr.com/photos/endymion120/

Chapter 5 - By: Phil Manker
https://www.flickr.com/photos/philmanker/

Chapter 6 - By: Joel Kramer
https://www.flickr.com/photos/75001512@N00/

Chapter 7 - By: iMorpheus
https://www.flickr.com/photos/sfj/

Chapter 8 - By: Carl Carpenter
https://www.flickr.com/photos/carlc/

Chapter 9 - By: Leo Reynolds
https://www.flickr.com/photos/lwr/

Chapter 10 - By: Extra Medium
https://www.flickr.com/photos/johnmueller/

Chapter 11 - By: Rob Watling
https://www.flickr.com/photos/robwatling/

Chapter 12 - By: Tim Dorr
https://www.flickr.com/photos/timdorr/

Other Books By The Author

Product Management

- How Product Managers Can Grow Their Career: How Product Managers Can Find And Succeed In The Right Job

- Product Management Secrets: Techniques For Product Managers To Boost Product Sales And Increase Customer Satisfaction

- Product Development Lessons For Product Managers: How Product Managers Can Create Successful Products

- Customer Lessons For Product Managers: Techniques For Product Managers To Better Understand What Their Customers Really Want

- Product Failure Lessons For Product Managers: Examples Of Products That Have Failed For Product Managers To Learn From

- Communication Skills For Product Managers: The Communication Skills That Product Managers Need To Know How To Use In Order To Have A Successful Product

- How To Have A Successful Product Manager Career: The Things That You Need To Be Doing TODAY In Order To Have A Successful Product Manager Career

- Product Manager Product Success: How to keep your product on track and make it become a success

Public Speaking

- Plan For Success: How To Plan Your Next Speech: How to plan a speech in order to achieve your goals and delight your audience

- How To Become A Better Speaker By Changing How You Speak: Change techniques that will transform a speech into a memorable event

- How To Give A Great Presentation: Presentation techniques that will transform a speech into a memorable event

- How To Rehearse In Order To Give The Perfect Speech: How to effectively rehearse your next speech to that your message be remembered forever!

- Secrets To Creating The Perfect Speech: How to create a speech that will make your message be remembered forever!

- Secrets To Organizing The Perfect Speech: How to organize the best speech of your life!

- Secrets To Planning The Perfect Speech: How to plan to give the best speech of your life

- How To Show What You Mean During A Presentation: How to use visual techniques to transform a speech into a memorable event

CIO Skills

- Technology That Every CIO Needs To Know About: How CIOs Can Stay On Top Of the Changes in the Technology That Powers the Company

- What CIOs Need To Know About Working With Partners: Techniques For CIOs To Use In Order To Be Able To Successfully Work With Partners

- Critical CIO Management Skills: Decision Making Skills That Every CIO Needs To Have In Order To Be Able To Make The Right Choices

- How CIOs Can Make Innovation Happen: Tips And Techniques For CIOs To Use In Order To Make Innovation Happen In Their IT Department

- CIO Communication Skills Secrets: Tips And Techniques For CIOs To Use In Order To Become Better Communicators

- Managing Your CIO Career: Steps That CIOs Have To Take In Order To Have A Long And Successful Career

- CIO Business Skills: How CIOs can work effectively with the rest of the company!

IT Manager Skills

- How IT Managers Can Make Innovation Happen: Tips And Techniques For IT Managers To Use In Order To Make Innovation Happen In Their Teams

- Staffing Skills IT Managers Must Have: Tips And Techniques That IT Managers Can Use In Order To Correctly Staff Their Teams

- Secrets Of Effective Leadership For IT Managers: Tips And Techniques That IT Managers Can Use In Order To Develop Leadership Skills

- IT Manager Career Secrets: Tips And Techniques That IT Managers Can Use In Order To Have A Successful Career

- IT Manager Budgeting Skills: How IT Managers Can Request, Manage, Use, And Track Their Funding

Negotiating

- Learn How To Signal In Your Next Negotiation: How To Develop The Skill Of Effective Signaling In A Negotiation In Order To Get The Best Possible Outcome

- Learn The Skill Of Exploring In A Negotiation: How To Develop The Skill Of Exploring What Is Possible In A Negotiation In Order To Reach The Best Possible Deal

- Learn How To Argue In Your Next Negotiation: How To Develop The Skill Of Effective Arguing In A Negotiation In Order To Get The Best Possible Outcome

- How To Open Your Next Negotiation: How To Start A Negotiation In Order To Get The Best Possible Outcome

- Preparing For Your Next Negotiation: What You Need To Do BEFORE A Negotiation Starts In Order To Get The Best Possible Deal

Miscellaneous

- Software Defined Networking: Design and Deployment, CRC Press 2014

- The Internet-Enabled Successful School District Superintendent: How To Use The Internet To Boost Parental Involvement In Your Schools

- Power Distribution Unit (PDU) Secrets: What Everyone Who Works In A Data Center Needs To Know!

- Making The Jump: How To Land Your Dream Job When You Get Out Of College!

"Technologies That IT Managers Can Use In Order To Make Their Teams More Productive"

> This book has been written with one goal in mind – to show you how an IT manager can build high performance teams. It's not easy being an IT manager so we're going to show you what you need to be doing in order create teams that can work together and deliver results!
>
> **Let's Make Your IT Career A Success!**

What You'll Find Inside:

- **Maybe it is Time for IT Leaders to Go Shopping to Learn New Tricks**

- **Just Whose Job Is Network Security Anyway?**

- **Why Cloud Computing Won't Work For Every IT Project**

- **IT Managers Need to Realize that Virtualization Isn't All That It's Cracked Up to Be**

Dr. Jim Anderson brings his 25 years of real-world experience to this book. He's been an IT manager at some of the world's largest firms. He's going to show you what you need to do (and not do!) in order to successfully manage your career!

www.ingramcontent.com/pod-product-compliance
Lightning Source LLC
Chambersburg PA
CBHW071805170526
45167CB00003B/1177